A TRUE BOOK™

SURVIVAL SKILLS

SHELTER

Diane Vukovic

Children's Press®
An imprint of Scholastic Inc.

SAFETY NOTE

This book suggests several survival skills techniques. When possible, they should all be done with adult supervision. Observe safety and caution at all times. The author and publisher disclaim all liability for any damage, mishap, injury, illness, or death that may occur from engaging in the survival skills techniques featured in this book or any other use of this book.

Special thanks to our content consultant, Ben McNutt, who has been teaching wilderness bushcraft and survival skills while leading remote expeditions to forest, jungle, desert, and frozen environments for more than 20 years. Ben also runs courses at wildhuman.com.

Library of Congress Cataloging-in-Publication Data
Names: Vukovic, Diane, author. | Francis, Kate, 1976– illustrator.
Title: Shelter / Diane Vukovic; illustrations by Kate Francis.
Description: First edition. | New York, NY: Children's Press, an imprint of Scholastic Inc., 2023. | Series: A true book: Survival skills | Includes bibliographical references and index. | Audience: Ages 8–10 | Audience: Grades 4–6 | Summary: "A new installment in the A True Book series focusing on Survival Skills"—Provided by publisher.
Identifiers: LCCN 2022022905 (print) | LCCN 2022022906 (ebook) | ISBN 9781338853766 (library binding) | ISBN 9781338853773 (paperback) | ISBN 9781338853780 (ebk)
Subjects: LCSH: Wilderness survival—Juvenile literature. | Survival—Juvenile literature. | BISAC: JUVENILE NONFICTION / Sports & Recreation / Camping & Outdoor Activities | JUVENILE NONFICTION / General
Classification: LCC GV200.5 .V857 2023 (print) | LCC GV200.5 (ebook) | DDC 613.6/9—dc23/eng/20220613
LC record available at https://lccn.loc.gov/2022022905
LC ebook record available at https://lccn.loc.gov/2022022906

10 9 8 7 6 5 4 3 2 1   23 24 25 26 27

Printed in China, 62
First edition, 2023

Design by Kathleen Petelinsek
Series produced by Spooky Cheetah Press

313930410224460

Find the Truth!

Everything you are about to read is true *except* for one of the sentences on this page.

Which one is **TRUE**?

T or F   A quinzee is a good shelter in hot climates.

T or F   A sloped A-frame is the warmest type of debris shelter.

Find the answers in this book.

What's in This Book?

These two basic items—a tarp and rope—are essential adventuring tools.

The **BIG** Truth

Stay calm if you get lost. Someone will find you!

Lost in the Woods

A snow shelter can keep you warm in very cold climates.

5

Surviving the Elements

Rabbits dig burrows, bear cubs and fox kits sleep in dens, and most **birds build nests.** Animals make shelters to **protect themselves** from the elements—like cold, heat, wind, and rain. Shelters also protect animals from predators. These are some of the same reasons humans have always sought shelter.

Most modern humans don't have to build their own shelters to live in. But **shelter-making** is still considered one of the most **important survival skills** to know.

According to the **survival rule of threes,** a person can live three weeks without food and three days without water—but only **three hours without shelter** in harsh environments. Hopefully, you will never need to use these skills. But if you are ever **lost in the wilderness,** knowing how to make a shelter **could save your life.**

Humans have been making shelters for at least 400,000 years!

Practicing skills for living in the wilderness is called "bushcraft."

You should practice making a shelter for fun. Then you will be prepared in case there is an emergency.

Understanding Survival Shelters

There are many different types of survival shelters, but they all have a few things in common. Survival shelters are simple structures that can be made quickly using whatever materials are available. That might be branches and leaves you collect from the ground, a tarp and rope that you brought with you, or even piles of snow. A survival shelter isn't supposed to be comfortable. Its purpose is to keep you safe until you can be rescued!

The body loses approximately 10 percent of its heat through the head, so be sure to wear a hat in cold weather!

Always be prepared! Know what the weather will be before you set off on an adventure.

Staying Warm

One of the main purposes of a survival shelter is to provide warmth. In cold temperatures, the body loses most of its heat through **radiation**. That is the process through which heat moves away from your body and into the colder air. A shelter with lots of **insulation** traps your body heat inside so you can stay warm. It takes longer to heat up a large shelter, so survival shelters should be small. The body loses a lot of heat when the wind blows, so a shelter should also protect against wind.

Using the Garbage Bag Trick

As water **evaporates** from a surface, it decreases the temperature of that surface. That is why sweating cools us down on hot days. But when it is cold outside, getting wet makes us feel even colder, and our bodies lose energy trying to stay warm. You need that energy to survive, so staying dry is crucial! If you do get wet and can't dry off, use this trick: Remove any soaking-wet clothes (leave them on if only damp). Then wrap yourself in a Mylar blanket or plastic tarp. If you don't have either of those, step into a trash bag and pull it up to your shoulders. Because water can't pass through the plastic, it won't evaporate and you will stay warm.

Your body loses heat faster in wet clothes than in dry.

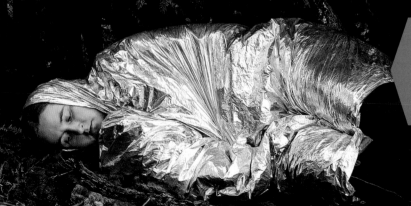

A Mylar emergency blanket is a helpful piece of camping gear. It is easy to carry and can keep you warm.

Where to Build Your Survival Shelter

Before you build your survival shelter, first look for natural shelters like caves or rock overhangs. If you see signs that animals might be using these areas, find another spot. If you can't find a natural shelter nearby, choose a spot that has lots of building material like dead trees and leaves on the ground. Also try to choose a spot with a natural **wind break**. For example, an area with lots of trees protects against wind better than an open field does.

Timeline: Early Human Shelters

2.5 MILLION YEARS AGO
Early humans use caves and other natural shelters.

400,000 YEARS AGO
Remains of tree-branch huts found in France are the oldest known human-made shelters.

25,000 YEARS AGO
The oldest permanent human settlement ever found is in the Czech Republic. It contains huts made from mammoth bones.

10,000 YEARS AGO
People make adobe dwellings from sun-dried bricks.

Natural Dangers

Never leave food inside your shelter in bear country. Hang it far away in a tree.

Your shelter needs to be safe from natural dangers. Avoid building the shelter on a steep slope. Rocks could fall on you, and if it rains, your shelter could be washed away. Don't make a shelter right next to a water source, either. The water levels can rapidly rise and flood your shelter. Also avoid animal trails so no critters come to check out your food supply! Finally, look up. Are there any widow-maker trees nearby? If so, stay away! Widow-makers are trees with dead or broken branches that could fall on you.

5,000 YEARS AGO
Roundhouses made from stone are used in Britain.

700 CE
Earth lodges are used by Indigenous Peoples living on the Great Plains.

1200s
Cliff dwellings are used by Ancestral Pueblo peoples.

1800s
Sod houses are built by American settlers in regions without trees.

Simple Survival Bed

Heat always moves toward cold. If you lie on the cold ground, the ground will suck the heat out of your body. That is why a survival bed is an important part of your shelter. The simplest way to make a survival bed is to pile up lots of fluffy **debris,** such as dead leaves, dry grass, and pine needles. When you lie on top of the debris, it acts as insulation against the cold ground. You can also snuggle into the debris like a natural sleeping bag so your body heat doesn't get lost into the air. If you are lost with a friend, make the bed wide enough for both of you.

To protect your hands as you collect debris, gather a handful of sticks to make a "broom." Or use your socks for gloves!

Pine needles make soft bedding.

14

Raised Survival Bed

If it is very cold or wet out, make a raised survival bed. The frame lifts your body off the ground, so it keeps you warm and dry.

BUILDING A RAISED SURVIVAL BED

1. Find two long, thick branches to use as the sides—or rails—of your bed frame. Lay them side by side on the ground where you're going to make your shelter. Leave enough room between the rails for your body.

2. Use your broom to rake a pile of debris from the ground and place it between the bed rails.

3. Lay smaller branches sideways from one rail to the other. This is where you will lie down.

4. Add more debris on top of the bed to use as a "sleeping bag." The more debris you add, the warmer you will be.

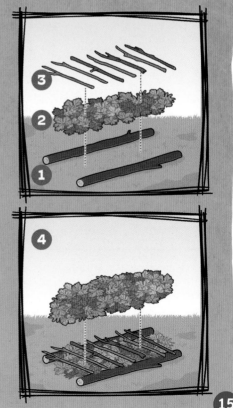

Don't damage living trees when practicing survival skills.

There are several types of debris shelters. This one is called a Lean-to.

Debris Shelters

Debris shelters are made out of natural materials that you find in the wilderness, such as branches, leaves, pine needles, and moss. This is the type of shelter you would make if you were lost and didn't have any supplies. There are several ways to make debris shelters, but they all include the same basic elements. A **ridgepole** serves as the backbone of the shelter. Branches are added to make "ribs." Finally, layers of debris are added on top to complete the walls.

Sloped A-Frame Shelter

The sloped A-frame shelter is usually considered the best for survival because it traps heat and blocks wind well. It gets its name because the entrance looks like the letter *A* and the ridgepole slopes down in the back. Remember to make your survival bed before constructing the shelter. The shelter needs to be wide enough to fit the bed.

You'll need to gather a lot of materials to make your shelter.

BUILDING A SLOPED A-FRAME SHELTER

1 Find a ridgepole that is at least 1 to 2 feet (0.3 to 0.6 meters) longer than your body and strong enough so it won't break under the weight of the shelter.

Ridgepole

Entrance

2 Prop up one side of the ridgepole so it is about waist height. You can prop it on a tree stump or tree branch. Or you can put two sticks together as indicated in the photo to make a base for the ridgepole. This will be the entrance to your shelter. The entrance should be pointed away from the wind.

Check the length of your ridgepole to make sure it is long enough for you to fit inside the shelter.

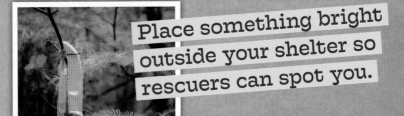

Place something bright outside your shelter so rescuers can spot you.

3 Gather lots of long sticks and lean them against the ridgepole to create ribs. Space the walls wide enough at the bottom so they fit around your bed. Don't make the shelter too big, though, or it won't warm up.

Ridgepole

Ribs

4 Collect lots of small sticks and branches. Place them side by side, close together on the ribs. The goal is to cover the frame as much as possible so debris won't fall through the ribs.

Try not to leave a lot of space between the sticks when building the walls.

Snakes often hide in debris, so be careful when grabbing sticks.

5. Place debris on top of the sticks until the whole shelter is covered. Pile lots of debris along the edges of the shelter to keep out the wind.

6. Make a big pile of debris in front of the entrance. Crawl into the shelter and then pull the debris toward you to plug the entrance.

The thicker you pile on the debris, the warmer and drier your shelter will be.

Debris Shelter Variations

Two popular variations on the sloped A-frame are the A-frame and Lean-to.

In an A-frame shelter, the ridgepole is propped up at both sides. Because it is bigger than a sloped A-frame, the shelter isn't as warm. It's often easy to find a natural ridgepole for this shelter, such as a fallen tree.

A Lean-to shelter provides protection only on one side, so it doesn't trap heat well. However, you would choose this shelter type if you wanted to make a fire to keep you warm. It isn't safe to make a fire in enclosed shelters.

A-frame

Lean-to

Are Tepees Good Survival Shelters?

Tepees, or tipis, are closely associated with Indigenous Peoples who lived on the Great Plains. Although members of these groups no longer live in tepees, they still consider the tepee an important symbol of their identity and heritage. In the past, tepees were ideal shelters for these **nomadic** people who followed bison herds across the plains. That is because the shelters could be set up and taken down quickly. However, tepees generally do not make good survival shelters. It is difficult to find enough long branches to make the tepee frame. It is also hard to get debris to stay on the slanted walls of a tepee. (Indigenous Peoples covered their tepees with animal skins). So, make a tepee for fun, but don't count on it for survival!

An average tepee weighed more than 500 pounds (227 kilograms)!

23

A tarp can also be used to catch rainwater and funnel it into a container.

Tarp shelters can be assembled quickly.

Tarp Shelters

There is a lot of gear you can use to make a shelter, but the most basic elements are a tarp and rope. Both items are light weight, so they are easy to carry on a hiking trip, and you can use them to make several types of survival shelters. Tarp shelters are faster to make than debris shelters and do a better job of blocking rain.

Tying a Ridgeline

Instead of using a ridgepole for your shelter, use rope to make a **ridgeline**. First, tie your ridgeline to two sturdy anchors, such as two trees. Make sure the trees are far enough apart that you can lie down between them. The ridgeline needs to be stretched very tight so it doesn't sag when you put the tarp on it. To do this, you can use an adjustable knot called the taut-line hitch.

HOW TO TIE A TAUT-LINE HITCH

1 Pass the end of the rope around the anchor. Then pass the short end of the rope through the long end.

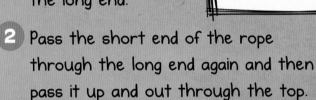

Short end

Long end

2 Pass the short end of the rope through the long end again and then pass it up and out through the top.

3 Bring the short end of the rope beyond the loops you just made. Pass it around the longer end one more time.

Start the last loop here

4 Pull the end of the rope until the knot is tight. Slide the knot back and forth to adjust the tension of the long end of the rope.

Forgot to pack rope?
Use your shoelaces!

Hanging the Tarp

Place the tarp over the ridgeline. For an A-frame shelter, the middle of the tarp needs to be centered on the ridgeline. There are lots of different ways to lay out the tarp, though. If the ground is wet or muddy, you can use the body bag or C-fly wedge. With these setups, part of the tarp is folded underneath you to make a floor.

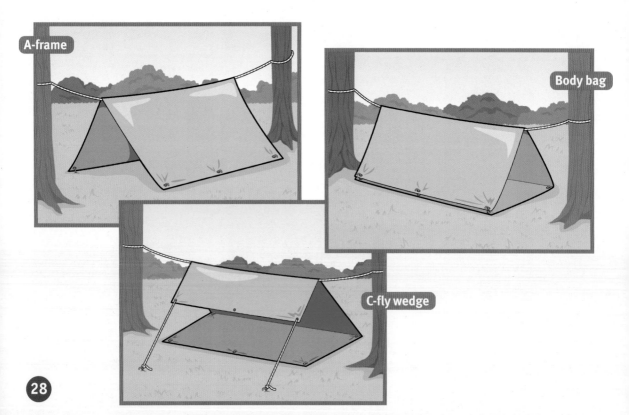

You can use pointy sticks and a rock instead of stakes and a hammer.

Remember to secure the walls of your shelter so you can stay warm and dry.

Once your tarp is positioned on the ridgeline, pull the sides out to make walls and secure them in position. You can do this by putting stakes through the tarp **grommets** and hammering them into the ground. If your tarp doesn't have grommets, you can fold a rock into the tarp and tie a knot around it to make an attachment point. As a last resort, use rocks or other heavy objects to hold the walls in position.

Lost in the Woods

efore going on outdoor adventures, do the smart thing: Tell
omeone where you are going and when you will come back. If you
on't come back when expected, that person will know to alert
earch and Rescue (SAR). There are lots of ways SAR can find you—
ke using scent-finding dogs, helicopters, and even drones! There
re a few simple things you can do to make the rescuers' job easier.

R finds 85 percent of lost
ple within 12 hours and
percent within 24 hours.

1

STOP

STOP stands for **S**tay calm,
Think, **O**bserve, and **P**lan. Staying
calm prevents bad decisions.
Think about how you got where
you are and observe the area
around you. Do you recognize any
landmarks? Are there any trail
signs? Based on this info, you can
plan what to do next.

Set Your Priorities

Immediately attend to your survival priorities. Are you injured? If so, first aid should be your top priority. If not, start building your shelter right away—it can take several hours. Signal for help as you work. "Three" is the universal signal for help. If you have a whistle, blow on it three times in a row. Pause and then repeat. If you don't have a whistle, bang on something that will make a lot of noise. You can also flash a mirror three times or build three fires in a triangle formation.

Hug a Tree

That means you should stay in one place until help arrives. Moving around will make it harder for SAR to find you, and it increases the likelihood that you'll get injured. Humans also have a tendency to walk in circles when lost, so walking in hopes of finding a landmark isn't a good idea. Unless you have a clear reason for moving and are confident in your navigation skills, just stay put!

Before going to the moon, Apollo 11 astronauts practiced survival skills in the desert.

A desert is an area that receives less rainfall than it loses through evaporation. Some deserts, like the one pictured here, are hot and sandy. Others are cool, or even covered with ice.

Shelters in Extreme Climates

The weather in extreme climates rapidly takes a toll on your body. In cold temperatures, you risk **frostbite** and **hypothermia**. In hot climates, you can suffer from dehydration, which is when your body fluids are depleted, or heat stroke. Heat stroke occurs when your body temperature gets too high. It can be life-threatening. To survive these extremes, you must be able to build a shelter very quickly, which is why it is especially important to bring the right gear with you.

Snow Cave and Quinzee

A snow cave

Snow is surprisingly good at holding in heat and can be used to make a warm shelter. You need at least 4 feet (1.2 m) of snow to dig a snow cave. If the snow isn't very deep, make a quinzee instead. It takes a long time to make snow shelters by hand, and your fingers would get cold. So you should always have a shovel in your emergency gear when adventuring in snow (see page 37).

A quinzee

Snowshoes make a good improvised shovel!

BUILDING A SNOW CAVE OR QUINZEE

1 Look for a deep snowdrift, preferably on a hill so you can dig straight into it to make a snow cave. Otherwise, shovel snow into a pile at least 4 feet (1.2 m) deep to make a quinzee. Stomp down the snow so it won't collapse as you dig.

(Quinzee)

2 A snow cave and quinzee are made the same way. The only difference is the entrance. For a snow cave, dig a short tunnel that leads into the main room. For a quinzee, dig a hole your body can fit through.

(Quinzee)

3 Then, carve out the inside of your snow cave or quinzee. Start by digging up and in to carve out a dome-shaped ceiling. If you try to carve the bottom of the shelter first, the weight of the snow on top will cause the shelter to collapse. The walls need to be at least 1 foot (0.3 m) thick, so stop digging if you see light through the walls.

(Quinzee)

4 Smooth out the ceiling. This prevents water from dripping on you as your body heat causes the snow to melt.

5 Use a long stick to poke a hole in the ceiling so fresh air can get in. Check your vent regularly and be sure to always keep it clear.

(Quinzee)

Tree-Pit Shelter

A tree-pit shelter is another type of snow shelter. It isn't as warm as a snow cave, but it is easier and faster to build—especially if you don't have a shovel. You just need to find the right kind of evergreen tree.

BUILDING A TREE-PIT SHELTER

1. Try to find an evergreen tree with long, low-hanging branches.

2. Dig a deep hole in the snow around the trunk. It should be at least 3 feet (0.9 m) deep.

3. Widen the pit, packing the snow outward to make a room.

4. Place broken evergreen branches on the floor. You can also place branches above the pit to make a ceiling.

Emergency Gear

When going into the wilderness, you should hope for the best but plan for the worst. Part of planning is bringing emergency gear. Pack a tarp, rope, flashlight, fire-starting kit, map and compass, first aid kit, whistle, and rain jacket or poncho, plus extra food and water. In winter, you'll need gear for melting snow, hand-warmer packets, spare gloves and socks, and, of course, a shovel! Your clothes are your first line of defense against the elements, so it's important that you dress properly for your adventure. No matter what time of year it is, avoid wearing cotton. It absorbs moisture and takes a long time to dry. Instead, wear layers of synthetic or wool clothing.

A folding shovel is a great tool to take on a hike. It is lightweight and compact.

Hot Desert Shelter

To make a shelter for a hot desert, you will need two tarps. The tarps are set up with a gap between them. The air in the gap keeps the sun's heat and UV rays from getting through during the day.

BUILDING A DESERT SHELTER

1. Secure four tall sticks in the ground.

2. Pass your rope through the grommets on the first tarp and tie it to the sticks. It needs to be high enough for you to fit underneath, about 18 inches (46 centimeters) from the ground.

3. Tie the second tarp 1 foot (.3 m) above the first.

4. Secure the sticks to heavy objects, like rocks.

As long as you know the basic setup for any survival shelter, you'll be able to adjust the shelter based on the materials you have on hand. With a bit of knowledge and creative thinking, you can make a survival shelter anywhere from almost anything!

5 If you don't have two tarps, you can also use one tarp folded in half, towels, or any other long material available. Instead of sticks, you can use stacked rocks.

LOST TEEN SURVIVES
by Building a Snow Cave

Robert Waldner spent several hours in the freezing cold after he got lost.

When 17-year-old Robert Waldner got lost on Mica Mountain in British Columbia, Canada, he made several smart decisions: He stayed calm, stayed put, and made a shelter.

Robert's ordeal had started with a family snowmobiling trip.

Not realizing that his dad and brother had stopped to fix a stalled snowmobile, Robert sped ahead and found himself lost in unfamiliar terrain. Realizing that backtracking would probably get him more lost, Robert decided to stay put. He was very cold and realized he needed a shelter to stay warm. Luckily, Robert had a shovel with him and used it to dig out a snow cave. He made sure to put the snowmobile in a clearing so it would be a signal for rescue helicopters.

Robert's family also made a smart decision. After searching for two hours, they were tired and running out of fuel for their snowmobiles. They realized that continuing the search on their own would put them at risk of getting lost, too. They called local Search and Rescue for help. Less than five hours later, the experts from South Cariboo SAR found Robert and took him home.

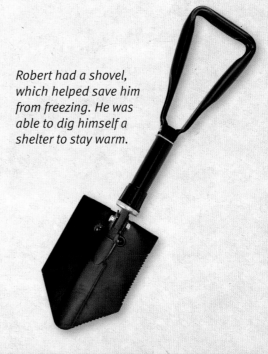

Robert had a shovel, which helped save him from freezing. He was able to dig himself a shelter to stay warm.

Use what you learned in this book to answer the questions below.

1 According to the survival rule of threes, how long can humans go without shelter?

2 Which location is safer for making a shelter?

A

B

3 Name the three main types of snow shelters shown here.

A

B

C

4 What is the most basic shelter-making gear?

5 What's the difference between a ridgepole and ridgeline?

6 **Name these different tarp shelters.**

A

B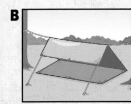

C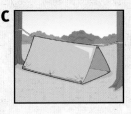

7 **In a survival situation, what does STOP stand for?**

8 **What are your survival priorities when lost?**

9 **What is the best gear for making a snow shelter?**

10 **Which of these items could you use to make a shelter?**

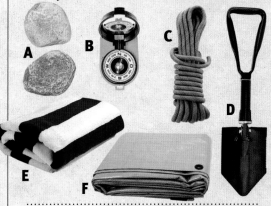

A B C D E F

11 **Which of these could you use to build a debris shelter?**

A B C D

True Statistics

Heat lost through the head: 10% of total body heat

Body temperature at which hypothermia occurs: 95°F (35°C)

Number of wilderness search and rescue operations in the United States each year: More than 50,000

Length of average search and rescue operation: 10 hours

Number of whistle blasts to signal for help: 3

Strongest common rope material: Nylon; approximately two times stronger than cotton rope of the same density

Air content of snow: 90%

Hottest recorded temperature on Earth as of July 2022: 134°F (57°C) recorded at Death Valley in 1913

Coldest nonpolar desert in the world: Gobi Desert with record lows of -40°F (-40°C)

Did you find the truth?

F A quinzee is a good shelter in hot climates.

T A sloped A-frame is the warmest type of debris shelter.

Resources

Other books in this series:

You can also look at:

Fears, Wayne J. *The Scouting Guide to Survival: Staying Warm, Building a Shelter, and Signaling for Help*. New York: Skyhorse, 2018.

Long, Denise. *Survivor Kid: A Practical Guide to Wilderness Survival*. Chicago: Chicago Review Press, 2011.

Winner, Cherie. *Ranger Rick Kids' Guide to Camping: All You Need to Know About Having Fun in the Outdoors*. Lake Forest, California: Quarto Publishing Group, 2017.

Glossary

debris (duh-BREE) the pieces of something that has been broken or destroyed; can refer to branches and leaves

evaporates (i-VAP-uh-rates) changes from a liquid into a vapor or gas

frostbite (FRAWST-bite) a condition that occurs when extremely cold temperatures damage parts of a person's body, such as fingers, toes, ears, or nose

grommets (GRAH-mets) pieces of firm material that strengthen an opening; can refer to a metal circle in the fabric of a tarp or tent

hypothermia (hye-puh-THUR-mee-uh) dangerously low body temperature

insulation (in-suh-LAY-shuhn) materials used to hold in heat

nomadic (noh-MAD-ik) describing a community of people that travels from place to place instead of living in the same place all the time

radiation (ray-dee-AY-shuhn) the giving off of energy in the form of light or heat

ridgeline (RIJ-line) a rope that is tied between two anchor points

ridgepole (RIJ-pohl) the horizontal pole at the top of a tent

wind break (WIND brayk) something that protects against the wind

Index

Page numbers in **bold** indicate illustrations.

About the Author

Diane Vukovic is an expert camper, backpacker, and disaster-preparedness specialist. It all started when she was a kid living in upstate New York and would spend her free time exploring the woods near her home, making forts and going on backpacking trips with her dad and sister. Now Diane has two daughters of her own and loves taking them on wilderness camping trips and teaching them survival skills like first aid and shelter-making. She also loves to travel to remote, lesser-known parts of the world and has been to more than 30 countries on six continents. Diane shares her knowledge at momgoescamping.com and primalsurvivor.net.